Explore the Bible®

Let the Word dwell in you.

With Explore the Bible, groups can expect to engage Scripture in its proper context and be better prepared to live it out in their own context. These book-by-book studies will help participants—

> grow in their love for Scripture;

> gain new knowledge about what the Bible teaches;

> develop biblical disciplines;

> internalize the Word in a way that transforms their lives.

Connect

@ExploreTheBible

facebook.com/ExploreTheBible

lifeway.com/ExploreTheBible

ministrygrid.com/web/ExploreTheBible

ISBN 978-1-4300-5675-3

Item 005695957

Dewey decimal classification: 222.8

Subject heading: NEHEMIAH\JERUSALEM—WALL\LEADERSHIP

ERIC GEIGER
Vice President, Church Resources

TONY EVANS
General Editor

TOBY JENNINGS
Managing Editor

JEREMY MAXFIELD
Content Editor

FAITH WHATLEY
Director, Adult Ministry

PHILIP NATION
Director, Adult Ministry Publishing

Send questions/comments to: Content Editor, *Explore the Bible: Adult Small-Group Study*; One LifeWay Plaza; Nashville, TN 37234-0152.

Printed in the United States of America

For ordering or inquiries visit *www.lifeway.com;* write to LifeWay Small Groups; One LifeWay Plaza; Nashville, TN 37234-0152; or call toll free 800.458.2772.

Page 7 quotation: Tony Evans, *Kingdom Man* (Carol Stream, IL: Tyndale, 2012), 19. Page 17 quotation: Tony Evans, Facebook, 1 December 2013 [cited 25 June 2014]. Page 27 quotation: Corrie Ten Boom, *Clippings from My Notebook* (Nashville: Thomas Nelson, 1982), 27. Page 37 quotation: Tony Evans, *Kingdom Man,* 43. Page 47 quotation: Ronald Reagan, "Remarks at the Annual National Prayer Breakfast," 3 February 1983 [cited 25 June 2014]. Available from the Internet: *www. reagan.utexas.edu/archives/speeches/1983/20383a.htm.* Page 57 quotation: Dietrich Bonhoeffer, BrainyQuote, cited 25 June 2014. Available from the Internet: *www. brainyquote.com.*

❯ ABOUT THIS STUDY

SOMETHING HAS TO BE DONE. SOMEONE HAS TO TAKE ACTION. WILL IT BE YOU?

God can make a difference through you. No problem is too big. No burden is too heavy. Nothing is too broken. Nobody is too lost. Nowhere is too far away. God is Lord of it all.

Change is possible. It's not easy, but it's possible.

The Book of Nehemiah gives great encouragement to anyone who sees what's wrong in the world and longs to fix it. It's a story of persevering and making the most of every opportunity. God uses people who are willing to take action for His sake.

Explore the Bible: Nehemiah helps you know and apply the encouraging and empowering truth of God's Word. Each session is organized in the following way.

UNDERSTAND THE CONTEXT: This page explains the original context of each passage and begins relating the primary themes to your life today.

EXPLORE THE TEXT: These pages walk you through Scripture, providing helpful commentary and encouraging thoughtful interaction with God through His Word.

OBEY THE TEXT: This page helps you apply the truths you've explored. It's not enough to know what the Bible says. God's Word has the power to change your life.

LEADER GUIDE: This final section provides optional discussion starters and suggested questions to help anyone lead a group in reviewing each section of the personal study.

❯ GROUP COMMITMENT

As you begin this study, it's important that everyone agrees to key group values. Clearly establishing the purpose of your time together will foster healthy expectations and help ease any uncertainties. The goal is to ensure that everyone has a positive experience leading to spiritual growth and true community. Initial each value as you discuss the following with your group.

❑ PRIORITY

Life is busy, but we value this time with one another and with God's Word. We choose to make being together a priority.

❑ PARTICIPATION

We're a group. Everyone is encouraged to participate. No one dominates.

❑ RESPECT

Everyone is given the right to his or her own opinions. All questions are encouraged and respected.

❑ TRUST

Each person humbly seeks truth through time in prayer and in the Bible. We trust God as the loving authority in our lives.

❑ CONFIDENTIALITY

Anything said in our meetings is never repeated outside the group without the permission of everyone involved. This commitment is vital in creating an environment of trust and openness.

❑ SUPPORT

Everyone can count on anyone in this group. Permission is given to call on one another at any time, especially in times of crisis. The group provides care for every member.

❑ ACCOUNTABILITY

We agree to let the members of our group hold us accountable to commitments we make in the loving ways we decide on. Questions are always welcome. Unsolicited advice, however, isn't permitted.

_____   _____

I agree to all the commitments.   Date

❯ GENERAL EDITOR

 **Dr. Tony Evans** is one of America's most respected leaders in evangelical circles. He is a pastor, a best-selling author, and a frequent speaker at Bible conferences and seminars throughout the nation.

Dr. Evans has served as the senior pastor of Oak Cliff Bible Fellowship in Dallas, Texas, for more than 35 years. He is also the founder and president of The Urban Alternative, a ministry that seeks to restore hope and transform lives through the proclamation and application of God's Word.

Dr. Evans is the author of more than 50 books, including the following LifeWay short-term Bible studies: *Victory in Spiritual Warfare, Kingdom Man, Kingdom Agenda, It's Not Too Late,* and *The Power of God's Names.* For information about these Bible studies, please visit *www.lifeway.com/tonyevans.*

› CONTENTS

Session 1   **God Inspires the Work** *(Nehemiah 2:1-8,17-18)* **6**

Session 2   **Establish Justice in God's Community** *(Nehemiah 5:1-13)*   **16**

Session 3   **Be Faithful in Adversity** *(Nehemiah 6:1-19)* **26**

Session 4   **Do Your Appointed Part** *(Nehemiah 7:1-7)* **36**

Session 5   **Get an Understanding** *(Nehemiah 8:1-12)* **46**

Session 6   **Commit Your Way to the Lord** *(Nehemiah 10:28-39)* . . .   **56**

Leader Guide **66**

GOD INSPIRES THE WORK

God restores His repentant people to do work that honors Him.

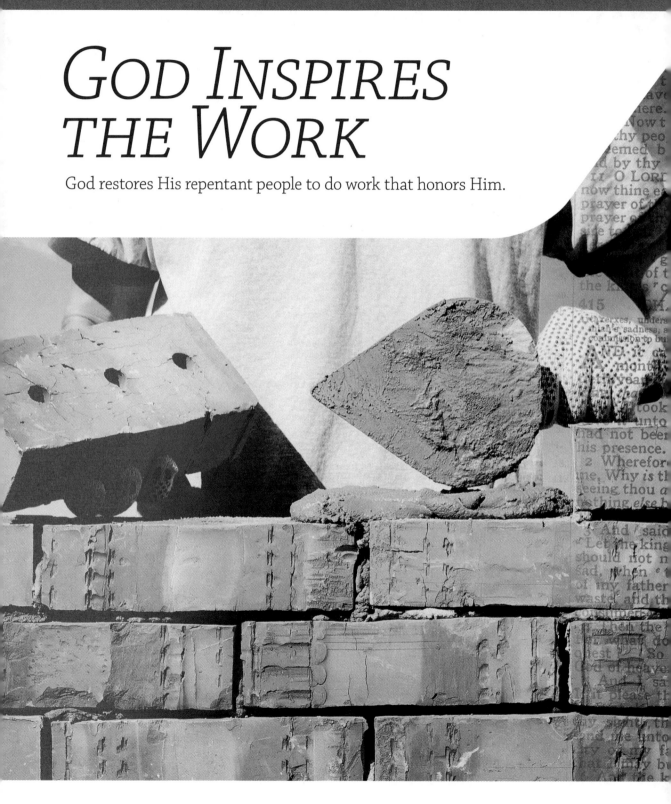

❯ ABOUT THE BOOK OF NEHEMIAH

In the fifth century B.C., during the height of the Persian Empire, a descendant of a sworn enemy of God's people rose to a position of great power in the empire. He used this position to plan and receive authorization for a genocide against the Jews, many of whom were living in exile in the heartland of the empire. (See the Book of Esther.)

The Sovereign God, however, had different plans for His exiled people. Through prophets such as Jeremiah and Ezekiel, the Lord God had declared that He would one day restore the covenant people to the promised land (see Jer. 33:7-9; Ezek. 36:24-28). This restoration would have political aspects, to be sure. But more important, God's people would be restored spiritually. The Lord would forgive their waywardness, draw them to Himself, and give them a new heart and spirit. They would be restored in their faith and in obedience to God's Word.

The Old Testament Books of Esther, Ezra, and Nehemiah chronicle events surrounding the Lord's restoration of Jewish exiles to the promised land. The books bear the names of three Jewish heroes of the faith—ordinary believers who accomplished extraordinary things as a result of God's mighty, providential hand and their bold, obedient faith.

AUTHOR

The Books of Ezra and Nehemiah contain sections that can be called memoirs, and those sections were most likely written by the two men. Yet most Bible scholars believe the books were brought into their final form by a single individual. Jewish tradition identifies that chronicler as Ezra, who is known from the text to have been a skilled scribe (see Neh. 8:1,9).

DATE

If the final compilation of Ezra-Nehemiah happened as described in the previous paragraph, then the date of writing logically followed soon after the close of Nehemiah's ministry in Jerusalem. Nehemiah went to Jerusalem to rebuild the wall in the 20th year of King Artaxerxes (444 B.C.; see 2:1). According to 13:6, Nehemiah returned to Babylon in the king's 32nd year, or around 432 B.C. Sometime later, Nehemiah requested and received a second leave of absence. He traveled to Jerusalem again, where he spent an undetermined amount of time leading the people in religious and social reforms (13:7-31). Thus, Bible scholars suggest that Ezra-Nehemiah was finalized around 430 B.C.

PURPOSE

Ezra-Nehemiah continues the history of God's people as told in 1–2 Chronicles. The restoration of Jewish exiles to the promised land highlights the Lord's faithfulness in keeping His promises. It also emphasizes the spiritual transformation needed by all people. Their stories can inspire us today as followers of Christ. Just as God showed His providential presence with and care for the Jewish exiles in the fifth century B.C., He continues to show His care for His people today. He continues to call believers to live boldly in faith, and He continues to provide servant leadership for His people.

NEHEMIAH 2:1-8,17-18

1 During the month of Nisan in the twentieth year of King Artaxerxes, when wine was set before him, I took the wine and gave it to the king. I had never been sad in his presence, **2** so the king said to me, "Why are you sad, when you aren't sick? This is nothing but depression." I was overwhelmed with fear **3** and replied to the king, "May the king live forever! Why should I not be sad when the city where my ancestors are buried lies in ruins and its gates have been destroyed by fire?" **4** Then the king asked me, "What is your request?" So I prayed to the God of heaven **5** and answered the king, "If it pleases the king, and if your servant has found favor with you, send me to Judah and to the city where my ancestors are buried, so that I may rebuild it." **6** The king, with the queen seated beside him, asked me, "How long will your journey take, and when will you return?" So I gave him a definite time, and it pleased the king to send me. **7** I also said to the king: "If it pleases the king, let me have letters written to the governors of the region west of the Euphrates River, so that they will grant me safe passage until I reach Judah. **8** And let me have a letter written to Asaph, keeper of the king's forest, so that he will give me timber to rebuild the gates of the temple's fortress, the city wall, and the home where I will live." The king granted my requests, for I was graciously strengthened by my God.

17 So I said to them, "You see the trouble we are in. Jerusalem lies in ruins and its gates have been burned down. Come, let's rebuild Jerusalem's wall, so that we will no longer be a disgrace." **18** I told them how the gracious hand of my God had been on me, and what the king had said to me. They said, "Let's start rebuilding," and they were encouraged to do this good work.

Think About It

Circle the different emotions Nehemiah exhibited and underline the issues prompting them.

What do these emotions suggest to you about Nehemiah?

› UNDERSTAND THE CONTEXT

I'M NOT THE HERO TYPE. HOW CAN I POSSIBLY MAKE A DIFFERENCE? SURELY SOMEONE ELSE COULD DO BETTER! HAVE YOU EVER HAD THOUGHTS LIKE THIS?

If so, you're not alone. Most of us have or will have them along the way. Very few people go through this life without at some point feeling unprepared—if not powerless—to make a difference. The real question is what we can do to move past those feelings.

The Book of Nehemiah picks up where the Book of Ezra ended. Jerusalem's wall had been toppled and torn apart in 586 B.C. as the people were taken into exile (see 2 Kings 25:10-11). Some 50 years later, a first group of exiles returned to Jerusalem and began to rebuild. Then Ezra led another group of exiles to Jerusalem in 458 B.C. Fourteen years later, however, an important task of restoration remained undone. The wall around Jerusalem lay in ruins.

Nehemiah lived in Susa in 445 B.C. He was still in exile, and he served as the cupbearer to King Artaxerxes. (This was the same king who had earlier commissioned Ezra's return to Jerusalem.) The royal cupbearer was one of the king's most trusted officials; he put his life on the line for the king every day. The cupbearer had a dual role: first, to taste whatever the king desired to drink, ensuring it was poison free; second, to provide security for the king's living quarters. Nehemiah's job wasn't menial; it was a role of influence and honor.

One day Nehemiah received a visit from a delegation of men from Judah (see Neh. 1:2). The men told him of the shameful state of affairs that continued to depress Jerusalem. Nehemiah was heartbroken. He fasted and prayed. He repented and pleaded with God to complete the restoration of His people (see 1:4-10). In the midst of his prayer, Nehemiah seemed to realize that he would have a part in what God was about to do. He also knew if God called him to serve, then God would have to make it possible for him to leave Susa. So Nehemiah prayed for grace and success while serving the king (see 1:11).

"WHEN GOD SEARCHES FOR A MAN TO ADVANCE HIS KINGDOM, DOES HE CALL YOUR NAME?"
—*Dr. Tony Evans*

› EXPLORE THE TEXT

DISTRESS EXPOSED *(Read Nehemiah 2:1-3.)*

Four months elapsed from the time Nehemiah received the news about Jerusalem until he had an opportunity to speak to the king. What did Nehemiah do during those four months? Nehemiah 1:4 suggests that he continued to pray and to look for an opportunity to help. We can also assume that he thought about ideas for getting the wall rebuilt—what materials would be needed, how to acquire them, and where to rally the workforce. He wanted be ready when God showed him the right moment to act.

That moment came during the month of Nisan (the first month on the Jewish calendar). Nehemiah was carrying out his normal duties as cupbearer. Wine had been delivered, so Nehemiah tested it before giving some to the king. He always performed this duty with a good attitude, because it was standard practice to enter the king's presence with a pleasant demeanor.

This time, however, the king recognized that his normally happy cupbearer was heartsick about something. A sudden wave of panic washed over Nehemiah. He had violated the cupbearer's code of conduct. It was an uncharacteristic lapse in his work ethic. But it was also an opportunity to trust God and to explain his situation to the king.

How can times of sadness or fear also become opportunities to grow in your faith?

Nehemiah opened his heart to the king. He first addressed the king with respect and then expressed his deep concern in the form of a question. The question gave the king latitude either to abruptly end the conversation or to graciously seek to help his heartsick servant.

Nehemiah referred to Jerusalem as the place where his ancestors were buried. Most ancient people groups treasured their ancestral burial grounds. A family's living members were responsible for preserving and maintaining the burial site. The king of Persia knew this, and he sympathized with Nehemiah's concern over the broken-down condition of his ancestral city.

Nehemiah carefully chose his words, framing his concern in nonpolitical and nonreligious terms. In doing so, he calmed any potential suspicions. Instead of immediately telling the king what he wanted to do, Nehemiah sparked the king's compassion and understanding.

What role should tactfulness play in a Christ follower's interactions with those who may not know Christ?

REQUEST PRESENTED

(Read Nehemiah 2:4-5.)

The king responded by asking Nehemiah to specify his request. But before Nehemiah spoke another word to the king, he prayed. The content of the prayer wasn't recorded, yet this prayer confirmed Nehemiah's deep faith. He had spent the past four months praying for God to act in a big way to help Jerusalem. Now God had put Nehemiah in a situation to have a conversation with the world's wealthiest, most powerful human ruler. And that ruler had just asked Nehemiah, in effect: "What do you want to do, and how can I help?"

What can we learn from Nehemiah about prayerful humility?

Nehemiah maintained a respectful, diplomatic tone to the king's authority. He knew his plan of action depended on the king's willingness to grant a leave of absence. Nehemiah further appealed to the king's favor. He asked the king to send him to Judah to rebuild the city of his ancestors—that is, Jerusalem. It was a huge, bold vision that in time would play a role in an even greater, God-sized plan. Jerusalem would one day be the place where salvation for sinners was accomplished through the substitutionary death and resurrection of Jesus Christ (see Matt. 20:17-19).

PREPARATIONS MADE (Read Nehemiah 2:6-8.)

The abrupt appearance in this verse of the queen sitting beside the king may indicate that this conversation was a separate, more private occasion than the one described in 2:1-5. In any case, the king wanted to learn a few additional details about Nehemiah's plan. In particular, he wanted to know how long Nehemiah would be away and when he could expect Nehemiah to return to Susa. Nehemiah specified a time of return, a fact that underscores the careful planning he had done over the previous months. We aren't told the time of return in this verse, but we learn from 5:14 and 13:6 that Nehemiah spent 12 years in Jerusalem before returning to Susa.

Constantly thinking ahead, Nehemiah sought to obtain written documents of authority that he knew he would need to travel safely through the outlying provinces and to complete his work in Jerusalem. History had already shown that non-Israelite groups around Judah would try to sabotage any attempts the Jews made to rebuild their covenant heritage (see Ezra 4:11-23). Nehemiah anticipated that he too would encounter resistance from the enemies of God's people.

Wall surrounding the old city of Jerusalem

Then Nehemiah requested a specific letter of authority to the official who had responsibility for the king's forest (likely the great cedar forests located in Lebanon, where prized timber was cut and sold all over the ancient world). The Jews under Zerubbabel had acquired timber from there to use in the rebuilding of the temple (see Ezra 3:7). Nehemiah wanted the timber for constructing the gates, stabilizing the wall, and building his residence.

The king granted all these requests. Yet Nehemiah, like Ezra, knew that neither he nor the king of Persia was the decisive player in the restoration of God's people. God was providentially at work, strengthening and using His willing servant Nehemiah.

How does Nehemiah's request for written documents from the king demonstrate a balance of taking personal responsibility and trusting God's sovereignty?

REBUILDING BEGUN *(Nehemiah 2:17-18)*

After arriving in Jerusalem and privately examining the conditions around the city (see 2:11-16), Nehemiah spoke to the citizens and challenged the people to rebuild. He identified with them and with the distress the city was experiencing. They needed the wall's physical protection for security. But it was the spiritual reality that distressed Nehemiah the most. The holy city was a disgrace. The crumbled wall was a reproach to the name of God, a matter of scorn and ridicule by Jerusalem's pagan neighbors. The honor of God's name was at stake.

In his effort to rally the people, Nehemiah reminded them of God's providence, protection, and sufficiency. God's hand, symbolic of His guidance and action, was evident. The king's words of permission and authority came next. This was acknowledged in the right order. The people were encouraged and committed themselves to the task ahead. Nehemiah's leadership, the people's partnership, and God's authority inspired them to work.

❯OBEY THE TEXT

Believers can pray and ask God for guidance when they're distressed over conditions in their communities. Christ wants His followers to be involved in His kingdom work. He helps them prepare and gives them opportunities to serve in His plan of redemption.

In what specific ways does our culture today directly or indirectly dishonor God?

What are you doing to prepare yourself to be used by God? What role does prayer have in that preparation? What can your group do to encourage one another to serve Christ?

What opportunities is God placing in front of you? What plan do you see Him working out in your life? What are you doing in response to His direction?

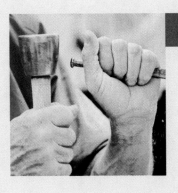

MEMORIZE

"The king asked me, 'What is your request?' So I prayed to the God of heaven" (Neh. 2:4).

Use the space provided to make observations and record prayer requests during the group experience for this session.

MY THOUGHTS

Record insights and questions from the group experience.

_____

_____

_____

_____

_____

_____

MY RESPONSE

Note specific ways you will put into practice the truth explored this week.

_____

_____

_____

_____

_____

MY PRAYERS

List specific prayer needs and answers to remember this week.

_____

_____

_____

_____

_____

ESTABLISH JUSTICE IN GOD'S COMMUNITY

God expects His restored people to treat every person with love and dignity.

❯ UNDERSTAND THE CONTEXT

YOU CAN ALWAYS FIND A TV SHOW ABOUT CRIME AND THE LAW. BUT THIS INTEREST IN JUSTICE IS NOT A NEW PHENOMENON.

The struggle between right and wrong is a story told throughout history. Nehemiah led the Jewish community in Jerusalem to renew their practice of true justice. They were in the middle of a great wall-building project. But living as the restored people of God meant more than laying stone blocks and building cedar gates. It meant living in community, treating one another right, and showing grace. A wall encircling a spiritually renewed people would provide security. That same wall around a people whose hearts were dens of greed and injustice would become a prison.

Nehemiah had come to Jerusalem on a mission (see Neh. 2:4-5). The overgrown piles of rubble that littered the landscape around the city were a source of shame for God's people. Nehemiah surveyed the situation and convinced the people to join him in rebuilding the city and its wall for God's glory (see 2:11-18).

Almost everyone got involved—men and women alike—with some families being assigned to repair the sections of the wall near their homes (see 3:1-32). As work progressed, however, opposition arose from the surrounding groups who were determined to sabotage the project (see 4:1-14). Nehemiah and the builders responded to the threat by strapping on their swords and organizing into shifts. Some worked, while others stood guard. If an attack came on one section, a quick trumpet blast rallied the people working elsewhere to come to the defense of their fellow citizens. Day and night Nehemiah and his staff stayed alert to these external threats (see 4:15-23).

Consequently, the next problem that arose must have felt like a sucker punch to Nehemiah. It wasn't a threat from without but rather from within. The intense, community-wide effort to rebuild the wall put an economic strain on families. To make matters worse, a famine ruined the crops. Money and food were scarce. Families grew so desperate that some parents sold their children into debtor's slavery. What galled Nehemiah the most about the situation was that some of the wealthy Jewish officials were taking advantage of their poor, desperate neighbors.

"FORGIVENESS IS NOT PRETENDING LIKE IT DIDN'T HAPPEN OR LIKE IT DIDN'T HURT. THAT'S CALLED LYING. FORGIVENESS IS A DECISION TO RELEASE A DEBT REGARDLESS OF HOW YOU FEEL."
—Dr. Tony Evans

› NEHEMIAH 5:1-13

1 There was a widespread outcry from the people and their wives against their Jewish countrymen. **2** Some were saying, "We, our sons, and our daughters are numerous. Let us get grain so that we can eat and live." **3** Others were saying, "We are mortgaging our fields, vineyards, and homes to get grain during the famine." **4** Still others were saying, "We have borrowed money to pay the king's tax on our fields and vineyards. **5** We and our children are just like our countrymen and their children, yet we are subjecting our sons and daughters to slavery. Some of our daughters are already enslaved, but we are powerless because our fields and vineyards belong to others." **6** I became extremely angry when I heard their outcry and these complaints. **7** After seriously considering the matter, I accused the nobles and officials, saying to them, "Each of you is charging his countrymen interest." So I called a large assembly against them **8** and said, "We have done our best to buy back our Jewish countrymen who were sold to foreigners, but now you sell your own countrymen, and we have to buy them back." They remained silent and could not say a word. **9** Then I said, "What you are doing isn't right. Shouldn't you walk in the fear of our God and not invite the reproach of our foreign enemies? **10** Even I, as well as my brothers and my servants, have been lending them money and grain. Please, let us stop charging this interest. **11** Return their fields, vineyards, olive groves, and houses to them immediately, along with the percentage of the money, grain, new wine, and olive oil that you have been assessing them." **12** They responded: "We will return these things and require nothing more from them. We will do as you say." So I summoned the priests and made everyone take an oath to do this. **13** I also shook the folds of my robe and said, "May God likewise shake from his house and property everyone who doesn't keep this promise. May he be shaken out and have nothing!" The whole assembly said, "Amen," and they praised the LORD. Then the people did as they had promised.

Think About It

Circle the words and phrases that relate to economic matters.

How did these economic matters affect the spiritual health of God's people?

› EXPLORE THE TEXT

A CRY FOR JUSTICE (Read Nehemiah 5:1-5.)

The people's great outcry didn't mark the beginning of the crisis. The pressure had been stewing beneath the surface for a while. Some Jewish families had paid a particularly heavy toll as their men spent days and nights in the city working on the wall. This forced many women into the fields and countryside to gather scarce food. A famine (see 5:3) made matters worse; desperate measures had to be taken just to survive. But worst of all was the injustice suffered by many families at the hands of other Jews.

God's covenant with Israel created a community based on wholehearted love for God (see Deut. 6:5) and unselfish love for neighbor (see Lev. 19:18). Jesus later explained that all the Law and the Prophets depended on these two commands (see Matt. 22:36-40). The offending Jews in Nehemiah's day were guilty of breaking the covenant. They not only turned a blind eye to their brothers and sisters in need but also heaped more misery on them. The nobles took advantage of others when they should have shown mercy.

What forms of widespread injustice do you see occurring today?

How do these forms of injustice compare or contrast with what was happening in Nehemiah's day?

At least three groups of people came to Nehemiah for help. The first group had large families with no food to eat. They, with their children, were going hungry. The reason for their impoverishment isn't specified, but the famine likely played a role. A second group included families who owned land but had been forced to mortgage everything they owned just to buy food. A third group complained of having to borrow money to pay the king's tax on their lands and vineyards.

When faced with a question about paying taxes to a foreign ruler, Jesus taught that God's people ought to give to Caesar what belonged to Caesar (see Luke 20:25; He went on to say that we're to give to God what belongs to God). Probably the crisis for the third group in Nehemiah's day had as much to do with being charged exorbitant interest rates on loans to pay the tax as with the tax itself.

At what point do certain practices go beyond good business to taking advantage of people's predicament?

Nehemiah 5:5 reveals the desperate nature of the crisis. Parents with no other options were having to consign their children to slavery. Although indentured service was a reality in biblical times, Israel's law provided for the just treatment of slaves and for their redemption (see Lev. 25:39-43).

The debt-ravaged families felt powerless. They and their children were as much a part of the covenant community as the nobles and officials were. Yet they were being oppressed, and their children had become other people's "property."

In what ways can the church be a voice for the powerless? Why are Christians responsible to stand for those who can't stand for themselves?

TAKING A STAND (Read Nehemiah 5:6-11.)

The outcry by desperate Jewish families stirred a different passion in Nehemiah. He became extremely angry. He was filled with righteous indignation on discovering that wealthier, more powerful citizens had taken advantage of their fellow Jews to the extent of forcing children into debtor's slavery.

Backed by the king's authority and flush with anger, Nehemiah could have immediately turned the tables on the offenders. He could have handed down severe punishment. Instead, he displayed bold, wise leadership. He took time to deeply consider the problem and its most God-honoring solution.

Next, Nehemiah confronted the offenders face-to-face. This took enormous courage, because these men were powerful members of the community. But they were breaking the covenant by charging interest on loans to fellow Jewish families. God's law forbade this practice within the covenant community (see Deut. 23:19-20).

Finally, Nehemiah called together a large assembly of citizens. The problem affected the entire community. The solution needed to include all the people too. The sin was public; repentance and restoration needed to be public as well.

Compare Nehemiah's actions to Jesus' teaching in Matthew 18:15-17. What are the similarities and differences?

KEY DOCTRINE
Christian Justice

All Christians are obligated to seek to make the will of Christ supreme in their lives and in society. Believers should work to provide for the orphaned, the needy, the abused, the aged, the helpless, and the sick, contending for the sanctity of human life from conception to natural death. Every Christian should seek to bring industry, government, and society as a whole under the sway of the principles of righteousness, truth, and brotherly love.

At the community assembly Nehemiah rebuked the offenders' actions on three counts.

1. By forcing Jewish families into debtor's slavery, the offenders were acting no differently than the exiles' foreign captors had acted.

2. The offenders' actions simply weren't right. Nehemiah appealed to the moral foundation of the covenant relationship, reminding them that God's people were to walk in the fear of God.

3. Nehemiah rebuked the offenders for staining Israel's testimony to the world as the people of God.

Nehemiah called on the offenders to follow his example. He too was a wealthy man with authority and had loaned money and grain to needy Jewish families. But Nehemiah challenged the offenders not only to stop collecting interest but also to return all the property and money they had confiscated.

How is a Christ follower's witness helped or hurt by the way he or she treats others?

ACTION PROMISED *(Read Nehemiah 5:12-13.)*

The offenders promised to return what had been taken as collateral and to erase the debts. Parents would now be reunited with their children. Families would no longer be homeless. Hungry people would have food to eat. And the Jewish community would once again enjoy God-given unity.

Nehemiah called on the priests to administer oaths as God's representatives. The oath was a promise made not only to one another but also to God. It was a serious step, done in public for all to see.

What promise have you made to God that you need to keep?

Who else might be drawn to praise God when you keep that promise?

Shaking out the folds of his outer garment (see 5:13) was symbolic of what Nehemiah asked God to do to all who failed to keep their oath. He asked God to shake out, or empty, the "pockets" of their robes of all possessions. This was essentially a warning about disobedience.

In response the congregation shouted "Amen," meaning *so be it.* Then they broke out in praise to God. God had led His people to move one step closer to restoration.

BIBLE SKILL
Evaluate a passage in light of a similar biblical event.

The needs of a group of people were called to Nehemiah's attention. Compare the situation recorded in Nehemiah 5:1-13 to the situation found in Acts 1:1-6.

How are the situations similar?

How are the situations different?

How does the Acts passage help you understand Nehemiah's actions?

❯ OBEY THE TEXT

Injustice is a symptom of a culture that devalues life. Believers are to stand up for the powerless, affirming the value of all people. Believers are called to build community by showing grace to others.

Do you agree or disagree with this statement: "Our group welcomes anyone who needs to experience the grace and love of Christ"? How can you strengthen this trait in your group?

What injustices do you observe in your community? How could you make others aware of these injustices? What other actions beyond awareness do you need to take?

Identify the person or people group in your community whom you have the most difficulty valuing. Ask God to help you overcome any prejudices you may have toward this person or group. Ask Him to show you one way you can demonstrate His love to this person or group.

MEMORIZE

"Acknowledge that Yahweh is God.
He made us, and we are His,—
His people, the sheep of His pasture"
(Ps. 100:3).

Use the space provided to make observations and record prayer requests during the group experience for this session.

MY THOUGHTS

Record insights and questions from the group experience.

_____

_____

_____

_____

_____

_____

MY RESPONSE

Note specific ways you will put into practice the truth explored this week.

_____

_____

_____

_____

_____

_____

MY PRAYERS

List specific prayer needs and answers to remember this week.

_____

_____

_____

_____

_____

_____

BE FAITHFUL IN ADVERSITY

God-given tasks can be completed with confidence and resolve because God has conquered all obstacles to His work.

› UNDERSTAND THE CONTEXT

IT'S BEEN SAID THAT A LEADER MUST HAVE THE HEART OF A WARRIOR, THE MIND OF A SCHOLAR, THE EYES OF AN EAGLE, AND THE HIDE OF A CROCODILE. A CHRISTIAN LEADER ADDS ANOTHER QUALITY TO THE LIST: THE FAITH OF A PROPHET. INDEED, IT'S A LEADER'S DEEP FAITH IN GOD THAT MAKES THE OTHER QUALITIES TRULY NOBLE.

"NEVER BE AFRAID TO TRUST AN UNKNOWN FUTURE TO A KNOWN GOD."
—*Corrie Ten Boom*

Servant-leaders lead from the front, not from behind. As a result, they're often the first ones to feel the brunt of an assault. Early-stage attacks may come in the form of verbal onslaughts—hurtful gossip, smear tactics, or outright lies. Leaders are sometimes blamed for bad things they didn't do and criticized for good things they tried to do. Too often they're misquoted, misunderstood, and never given an opportunity to set the record straight.

As a servant-leader, Nehemiah had to deal with some underhanded tactics by opponents. Jealous non-Israelite officials opposed his efforts to rebuild the wall around Jerusalem. However, Nehemiah's deep faith in God kept him (and the wall) on track.

Since humanity's fall in the garden of Eden, God's kingdom work has been done in a hostile environment. Jesus came into the world He created, but that world didn't always recognize or receive Him (see John 1:10-11). Both the Old and New Testaments depict the life of God's people as one of daily struggle against a powerful Enemy (see Dan. 7:17-22; Eph. 6:10-18).

The enemies of God's people in Nehemiah's day were of various backgrounds. Some groups—the people of Ammon, Arabia, and Ashdod, for example—had lived in the areas surrounding Judah for centuries. Other groups—the people of Samaria, for example—had been transplanted into the area as captives when Israel fell as a result of its rebellion against God (the Northern Kingdom to Assyria in 722 B.C., the Southern Kingdom to Babylon in 586).

Under the Persian Empire these surrounding groups strongly opposed the restoration efforts of the Jews who returned from exile. They determined to do whatever they could to sabotage the work of God's people. Consequently, Nehemiah found himself as a primary target of their verbal abuse, criticism, slander, and threats.

them;
you ca
part of
gather
will br
that I
name t
10 ° A
and thy
redeem
and by
11 O
tha
prayer
prayer
sire to
per, I p
day, an
the sig
the kin
415
A xerxes
miah's a.
commiss

▶ NEHEMIAH 6:1-19

1 When Sanballat, Tobiah, Geshem the Arab, and the rest of our enemies heard that I had rebuilt the wall and that no gap was left in it—though at that time I had not installed the doors in the gates— **2** Sanballat and Geshem sent me a message: "Come, let's meet together in the villages of the Ono Valley." But they were planning to harm me. **3** So I sent messengers to them, saying, "I am doing a great work and cannot come down. Why should the work cease while I leave it and go down to you?" **4** Four times they sent me the same proposal, and I gave them the same reply. **5** Sanballat sent me this same message a fifth time by his aide, who had an open letter in his hand. **6** In it was written: It is reported among the nations—and Geshem agrees—that you and the Jews plan to rebel. This is the reason you are building the wall. According to these reports, you are to become their king **7** and have even set up the prophets in Jerusalem to proclaim on your behalf: "There is a king in Judah." These rumors will be heard by the king. So come, let's confer together. **8** Then I replied to him, "There is nothing to these rumors you are spreading; you are inventing them in your own mind." **9** For they were all trying to intimidate us, saying, "They will become discouraged in the work, and it will never be finished." But now, my God, strengthen me. **10** I went to the house of Shemaiah son of Delaiah, son of Mehetabel, who was restricted to his house. He said: Let us meet at the house of God inside the temple. Let us shut the temple doors because they are coming to kill you. They are coming to kill you tonight! **11** But I said, "Should a man like me run away? How can I enter the temple and live? I will not go." **12** I realized that God had not sent him, because of the prophecy he spoke against me. Tobiah and Sanballat had hired him. **13** He was hired, so that I would be intimidated, do as he suggested, sin, and get a bad reputation, in order that they could discredit me. **14** My God, remember Tobiah and Sanballat for what they have done, and also Noadiah the prophetess and the other prophets who wanted to intimidate me. **15** The wall was completed in 52 days, on the twenty-fifth day of the month Elul. **16** When all our enemies heard this, all the surrounding nations were intimidated and lost their confidence, for they realized that this task had been accomplished by our God. **17** During those days, the nobles of Judah sent many letters to Tobiah, and Tobiah's letters came to them. **18** For many in Judah were bound by oath to him, since he was a son-in-law of Shecaniah son of Arah, and his son Jehohanan had married the daughter of Meshullam son of Berechiah. **19** These nobles kept mentioning Tobiah's good deeds to me, and they reported my words to him. And Tobiah sent letters to intimidate me.

Think About It

Underline words or phrases that point to Nehemiah's trust in God.

❯ EXPLORE THE TEXT

WHEN FALSELY ACCUSED
(Read Nehemiah 6:1-9.)

Powerful enemies opposed the Jews' wall-building project from the start. Tribal rulers maintained their power and wealth by making it their business to know everything that happened around them. If necessary, they acted swiftly and decisively to destroy the perceived threat. When Sanballat, Tobiah, and Geshem learned that the wall in Jerusalem was almost complete, they sprang into action. In their minds a restored Jewish people in a restored Jerusalem spelled nothing but trouble for the entire region.

Stopping the project meant stopping Nehemiah, the leader of God's people. So they sent Nehemiah an invitation to meet with them at Ono (about seven miles southeast of Joppa). But Nehemiah wasn't fooled. He knew from past experience with these men that they intended to harm him.

What thoughts run through your mind when you realize that someone wants to stop you from doing God's work?

Nehemiah placed priority on his work. This emphasis wasn't boastful but rather a statement of the project's importance. Nehemiah wasn't distracted or detoured from the priority of his calling. Four times the opponents sent an invitation; four times Nehemiah returned the same reply: the work was too important and the finish line too close to stop now.

Sanballat ramped up the pressure with a new tactic. He sent an open (unsealed) letter to Nehemiah by a messenger. This tactic was not only to insult Nehemiah but also to spread rumors about his personal ambitions. The letter stated two unfounded accusations. First, it accused Nehemiah and the Jews of planning to revolt against the Persian Empire. Geshem the

Arab was evidently the source of this accusation. Second, the letter charged that Nehemiah intended to become the Jews' new king. It further stated that Nehemiah had prophets standing by in Jerusalem who were ready to declare his kingship.

The letter's clincher was a not-so-veiled threat that the Persian king would hear about the charges. At the very least, the king would recall his cupbearer to Susa to answer the accusations. So Nehemiah was faced with a hard choice: either agree to meet with his opponents or face a recall (and perhaps worse) from the king of Persia.

Nehemiah responded boldly, denying the rumors and confronting his accusers with their true motives. They were trying to terrorize God's leader and God's people, thus attempting to sabotage the work of God's kingdom.

The kind of boldness Nehemiah displayed came as a result of his deep faith in the Lord. It came as he communed with God in prayer, asking for the strength that only God can give. Again and again, Nehemiah modeled the kind of prayer life needed by every follower of Christ. He prayed for God to bolster his courage in the midst of threats and false accusations. He prayed for strength to focus on the great work of God's kingdom rather than on his personal fears and needs.

What roles do faith and prayer play in your efforts to serve Christ?

WHEN PROMISED FALSE SECURITY
(Read Nehemiah 6:10-14.)

The next ploy of Nehemiah's accusers involved a Jewish prophet named Shemaiah [shih MAY uh]. Not all Jewish citizens were in favor of the building project, and this prophet seems to have been one of the naysayers. Sanballat and Tobiah hired him to frighten Nehemiah into violating God's calling concerning the temple.

Shemaiah was restricted to his house, which possibly means that he had confined himself to give Nehemiah the impression that the two of them were in imminent danger. Shemaiah suggested they hide inside the temple until the danger passed. To do so, however, would mean that Nehemiah would be disgraced by going where only priests were allowed. He would also be labeled a coward.

Again, Nehemiah saw through the ruse. The phrase "Should a man like me" (6:11) means that Nehemiah understood and accepted his responsibilities as a leader. A true captain doesn't abandon the ship when storms threaten. Neither does a godly leader abandon the work of God's kingdom out of personal fear. Nehemiah's faith and sense of responsibility prevented him from abandoning his post, especially to run and hide in the temple. He realized Shemaiah wasn't speaking from God but was only a hired conspirator.

Here again, Nehemiah showed himself to be a man of constant prayer. He was being lied about, lied to, and threatened, not by one person but by a host of individuals. The natural reaction would be to lash out in revenge against his enemies. But Nehemiah prayed, trusting God with the outcome (see Deut. 32:35; Rom. 12:19).

When have you been tempted to accept a false form of security instead of relying on God?

> **KEY DOCTRINE**
> *The Kingdom*
>
> The kingdom of God includes both His general sovereignty over the universe and His particular kingship over people who willfully acknowledge Him as King. Christians ought to pray and labor that the kingdom will come and God's will be done on earth.

WHEN FACTIONS ARISE *(Read Nehemiah 6:15-19.)*

Despite opposition, Nehemiah and the community of faith rebuilt the massive stone wall around Jerusalem in 52 days. Archaeologists estimate that the perimeter wall was 1½ miles around. The completion of the enormous project was a testimony to Nehemiah's exceptional, bold leadership and the community's willingness to persevere (see 4:6).

An account of the wall-dedication service appears in Nehemiah 12:27-43. It was a joyous occasion of worship, singing, and celebration. By contrast, the enemies of God's work (Sanballat and his conspirators) were stunned by the wall's completion. But the wall figured into God's ultimate plans for His people; thus, its completion was ensured.

What acts or events in your life would you point to as powerful testimonies of God's greatness?

Tobiah was identified in 2:10 as an Ammonite. The region of Ammon lay on the eastern side of the Jordan River. However, Tobiah had made many strategic agreements—political, financial, and marital—with some of the leading Jewish families living in Judah. Tobiah may even have been a nominal follower of Israel's God. In an effort to harass Nehemiah, he continued to correspond with the Jewish nobles after the wall's completion.

Through his associations Tobiah modified his tactics for a time from a frontal assault to a more covert campaign. He did favors (good deeds) for the nobles in return for their loyalty and for information about Nehemiah's activities. Consequently, the nobles always spoke well of Tobiah in Nehemiah's presence. But Nehemiah still wasn't fooled by Tobiah's overtures. As a result, Tobiah returned to the use of scare tactics delivered to Nehemiah in letters. Nehemiah would need to depend on God's encouragement and wisdom every day.

How can believers distinguish between genuine offers of friendship or cooperation and deceitful overtures?

BIBLE SKILL
Compare common experiences to gain insight.

Nehemiah faced opposition because of his obedience to God. He wasn't alone in facing opposition. Read 1 Peter 4:12-13.

How does this passage speak to Nehemiah's experience in Nehemiah 6?

How do Peter's principles and Nehemiah's experience give believers courage to face opposition?

❯ OBEY THE TEXT

People who seek to be obedient to God aren't immune from opposition. Faith and a consistent prayer life help believers discern true and false motives in themselves and in others. They also help believers stay focused on a God-given task for His honor.

Outline the steps you take when facing obstacles and opposition. What adjustments do you need to make to more closely align your approach with what you learned in this Bible study?

What God-given task have you worked on that was in danger of being derailed? What action did you take (or do you need to take now) to get that task back on track? How can you find support in your Bible study group to remain on track?

List the tasks you must complete in the next week. How can you trust God to help you complete the tasks identified? How can you give honor to God for each task you complete?

MEMORIZE

"I consider that the sufferings of this present time are not worth comparing with the glory that is going to be revealed to us" (Rom. 8:18).

Use the space provided to make observations and record prayer requests during the group experience for this session.

MY THOUGHTS

Record insights and questions from the group experience.

_____

_____

_____

_____

_____

_____

MY RESPONSE

Note specific ways you will put into practice the truth explored this week.

_____

_____

_____

_____

_____

_____

MY PRAYERS

List specific prayer needs and answers to remember this week.

_____

_____

_____

_____

_____

_____

DO YOUR APPOINTED PART

God uses each of His covenant people to accomplish His purposes.

» UNDERSTAND THE CONTEXT

HAVE YOU EVER MARVELED AT THE ROLE SOCIAL MEDIA PLAYS IN OUR WORLD TODAY? WHO WOULD HAVE IMAGINED EVEN A DECADE AGO THAT SUCH A PHENOMENON COULD HELP TOPPLE DICTATORS, BRING TERRORISTS TO JUSTICE, OR INFLUENCE MAJOR ELECTIONS? SOCIAL MEDIA MEANS WORLDWIDE CONNECTIVITY FOR MILLIONS OF HUMAN BEINGS.

In one sense, the success of social media shouldn't surprise us. We are intensely social creatures. God made us that way (see Gen. 2:18). We also learn rather quickly by experience that major achievements are rarely the result of a single person working in isolation. As the writer of Ecclesiastes pointed out, "Two are better than one because they have a good reward for their efforts. For if either falls, his companion can lift him up; but pity the one who falls without another to lift him up" (Eccl. 4:9-10).

Some tasks require the effort, coordination, and strength of many people working together. Ask any winning team, successful corporation, or growing church. A team working together can win championships. Coworkers who are focused on the same goals can outperform any one person. Likewise, a church in which all members serve by using their God-given gifts can effectively do their part in fulfilling Christ's command to make disciples of all nations.

Nehemiah challenged individuals in his day to do their part in God's kingdom work. Everyone was needed. Everyone had a part. Much of the workforce Nehemiah had called into action to build the wall actually lived in the surrounding regions of Judah. Chapter 3 reveals that workers from other areas came together with the inhabitants of Jerusalem to accomplish this work. Everyone had a job to do. But when the work was completed, most of the workers expected to return to their homes outside the city.

Nehemiah again displayed his God-given leadership qualities. He organized the city's administration and then set about to repopulate the city. God gave him a plan for that work. The plan is described in Nehemiah 11, a plan whereby all the surrounding towns and families enlisted 10 percent of their members to relocate to Jerusalem.

> "THE GREATEST PLAYER ON ANY TEAM, WHETHER A CORPORATE, FAMILY, MINISTRY, OR SPORTS TEAM, IS THE PLAYER WHO MAKES CERTAIN THAT HIS CONTRIBUTION BEST FITS WITHIN THE GOALS AND STRATEGIES OF THE TEAM."
> —*Dr. Tony Evans*

NEHEMIAH 7:1-7

1 When the wall had been rebuilt and I had the doors installed, the gatekeepers, singers, and Levites were appointed. **2** Then I put my brother Hanani in charge of Jerusalem, along with Hananiah, commander of the fortress, because he was a faithful man who feared God more than most. **3** I said to them, "Do not open the gates of Jerusalem until the sun is hot, and let the doors be shut and securely fastened while the guards are on duty. Station the citizens of Jerusalem as guards, some at their posts and some at their homes." **4** The city was large and spacious, but there were few people in it, and no houses had been built yet. **5** Then my God put it into my mind to assemble the nobles, the officials, and the people to be registered by genealogy. I found the genealogical record of those who came back first, and I found the following written in it: **6** These are the people of the province who went up among the captive exiles deported by King Nebuchadnezzar of Babylon. Each of them returned to Jerusalem and Judah, to his own town. **7** They came with Zerubbabel, Jeshua, Nehemiah, Azariah, Raamiah, Nahamani, Mordecai, Bilshan, Mispereth, Bigvai, Nehum, and Baanah.

Think About It

Circle the descriptions of Jerusalem's physical structures and their condition.

Underline the steps Nehemiah took after the city's wall was rebuilt.

In what ways did Nehemiah get others involved in the work?

❯ EXPLORE THE TEXT

A ROLE TO PLAY *(Read Nehemiah 7:1-3.)*

The Jews had accomplished a major feat in building the wall in a short period of time. Their construction role was finished; now their other roles back home needed to be resumed. Like a city that loses a major job-creating business, Jerusalem was about to face a whole new set of challenges.

Nehemiah took immediate action to strengthen the religious and civil organization within Jerusalem. First, the city and its temple needed a trustworthy security operation. Gatekeepers were guardians of the city gates and therefore controlled access to the city. Usually, the gatekeepers were watchmen or soldiers for the temple entrances, but Nehemiah extended their responsibilities to include the gates in the city wall. The gatekeepers essentially provided security for worshipers entering the temple.

Second, the city needed spiritual organization. So Nehemiah appointed temple singers to lead the community in the worship of God. He reminded the people that life was more than work. He appointed the singers to help worshipers make God their highest priority in the community.

Third, the city needed the regular, effective teaching of God's Word. So Nehemiah appointed the Levites to help instruct the people. Historically, the Levites often proved themselves to be devoted to God and His Word (see Ex. 32:26-29). They were consecrated to God, performing duties that included preparation for sacrifices, administrative responsibilities, and teaching people the Scriptures (see Num. 8:5-26).

In what ways do you see security and spiritual organization modeled in your church?

Nehemiah had promised the king of Persia that he would return to his duties in Susa at a definite time (see Neh. 2:6). Yet he didn't want to leave Jerusalem without putting in place a trustworthy civic organization to complement the spiritual organization. So he made two additional key appointments.

Hanani was Nehemiah's brother. He was among the group who first came to Susa to tell Nehemiah about Jerusalem's state of disgrace. Hanani's passionate concern for the city helped set in motion the whole course of Nehemiah's actions (see 1:2-3). Thus, any hint of bias here would be unfounded. Hanani was a man of courage and faith. He was a fit leader to be in charge of Jerusalem.

Nehemiah appointed Hananiah, the commander of Jerusalem's security forces, to serve alongside his brother. Hananiah would contribute strong military skills to protect the city from its enemies. But Hananiah, like Hanani, also possessed spiritual qualities that made him stand out above other potential leaders. Hananiah was a man of integrity. Both of these men, working together, would help ensure continued blessing for God's people where once there had been disgrace.

What qualities do you expect in public officials?

Which of those qualities would you also expect in church leaders?

What additional qualities would you expect in church leaders?

The wall wouldn't guarantee protection if its gates were left open and unguarded. So Nehemiah gave careful instructions to Hanani and Hananiah about the gates. First, Nehemiah instructed that the gates into the city should not be opened until the sun was hot. In other words, except in broad daylight all entrances to the city were to remain closed and barred. Enemies often attacked a walled city in the predawn hours when its defenses might be least prepared.

Nehemiah appointed two kinds of guards for the city. The first group was the official guards—the gatekeepers who patrolled the wall at specific stations. The second kind resembled citizen patrols. Residents of the city were appointed to keep watch near their homes. The wisdom in this approach is clear. Citizens mounted the wall opposite their houses, rotating the duty so that someone would be on guard at all times. Nehemiah had used a similar strategy during the wall's construction phase (see 4:13-17).

What are some ways every person in your group can play a role in guarding the group's well-being?

List specific names, needs, and opportunities in your group.

A PLACE TO BELONG (Read Nehemiah 7:4-7a.)

The city was extremely vulnerable to attacks without permanent residents. For years Jerusalem had lain in ruins and was largely uninhabited. Evidently, the returning exiles preferred to settle in the outlying areas that offered more stability, security, and land for cultivation. The statement "no houses had been built yet" (7:4) means no new houses had been constructed during or after the rebuilding of the wall.

In an effort to recruit families to relocate inside the city wall, Nehemiah assembled the people for a census. God had put an idea into his mind for solving the dilemma. Nehemiah faithfully prayed for God's wisdom and strength, and God was faithful to provide for Nehemiah (compare John 14:12-14).

The task of repopulating Jerusalem wouldn't be easy. Nehemiah was no longer organizing a temporary workforce; he was now asking people to uproot from familiar surroundings and move to a new locale—a place that required vigilance against danger. It would be a sacrifice for people to make such a move.

Nehemiah assembled the tribal leaders, officials, and the people to work out a plan. The plan, described in greater detail in Nehemiah 11:1-2, called for 10 percent of the local population to relocate inside the city. The plan wasn't coercive; those who relocated appear to have done so voluntarily and with the knowledge that they were part of something greater than themselves.

To recruit the volunteers, Nehemiah used a copy of a genealogical record he discovered. It was the list of all the families and groups who returned to Jerusalem with Zerubbabel in 538 B.C. Genealogies linked the Jews not only to the heritage of their past but also to the hope for their future. Nehemiah wanted to repopulate Jerusalem with citizens who knew they were Jews and were proud of it.

What about your past makes you who you are today?

BIBLE SKILL
Use a Bible atlas (print or online) to learn about places mentioned in Scripture.

Find a map showing the city walls of Jerusalem. Pay attention to the wall boundaries during the time of Ezra and Nehemiah, comparing the boundaries to earlier and later boundaries.

List ways the various boundaries help you understand the history of Jerusalem.

The word *province* (see 7:6) refers to Judah rather than to Babylon. Each family group returned to its original land. Doing so emphasized the continuing link between the former covenant community of Israel and the restored exiles. The people reaffirmed their past roots, connecting them with their present hopes.

The lengthy list of names represents more than 40,000 returnees. (The list is nearly identical to a list in Ezra 2.) The list of names emphasizes the importance of every believer's role in God's kingdom work. God wants to use all His people to accomplish His purposes.

How would you describe your current role in God's kingdom work?

How has God repositioned you to bring you to a place of usefulness?

❯ OBEY THE TEXT

God continues to call His people to do kingdom work. Each role or responsibility a believer carries out is important in advancing the gospel.

What role do you believe God wants you to fulfill in His service? What steps do you need to take to start doing your part or to improve in that service?

As a group, list actions that characterize a healthy Bible study group. Determine as a group the actions that need to be strengthened in your group. Pray that God will lead all individuals in the group to find their place to serve in kingdom work.

What one action will you take to begin or improve the use of your gifts and talents to advance the gospel?

MEMORIZE

"Whatever you do, do it enthusiastically, as something done for the Lord and not for men" (Col. 3:23).

Use the space provided to make observations and record prayer requests during the group experience for this session.

MY THOUGHTS

Record insights and questions from the group experience.

_____
_____
_____
_____
_____
_____

MY RESPONSE

Note specific ways you will put into practice the truth explored this week.

_____
_____
_____
_____
_____
_____

MY PRAYERS

List specific prayer needs and answers to remember this week.

_____
_____
_____
_____
_____
_____

GET AN UNDERSTANDING

Faith seeks understanding through regular and reverent hearing of God's Word.

› UNDERSTAND THE CONTEXT

DO YOU THINK AMERICA IS RIPE FOR ANOTHER GREAT AWAKENING? THIS TERM HAS AN IMPORTANT MEANING IN THE HISTORY OF THE UNITED STATES. IT DESCRIBES A PERIOD OF INTENSE, WIDESPREAD REVIVAL.

During an awakening, hosts of individuals and churches are awakened to a new enthusiasm for God, and positive changes usually occur in the general culture. We've witnessed at least three great awakenings in the United States: one in the mid-1700s, another in the early 1800s, and a third that ignited just before the Civil War and continued until the end of the 19th century.

Spiritual awakenings around the world throughout history appear to follow a similar pattern: a proclamation of God's Word, repentance of sin, prayer that acknowledges God's holiness, and a mobilization of God's people to obedient action. That pattern can be seen in Scripture as well. Nehemiah prayed for and worked toward the restoration of God's people, the Jews, after their return from exile. Part of that restoration involved rebuilding physical structures—the temple and the wall. More important, however, was the revival of the people's faith, a great awakening of their love for God (see Deut. 30:4-6).

When the walls were being restored, the spiritual condition of the people was often as bad as the broken walls. Ezra had come to Jerusalem 13 years before Nehemiah arrived. Ezra's passion was to study God's law, obey it personally, and teach it to God's people (see Ezra 7:10). Although Ezra isn't mentioned in the Book of Nehemiah until chapter 8, no evidence suggests he had left Jerusalem during Nehemiah's early years of leadership. A day came when God used Nehemiah and Ezra's leadership to spark a spiritual awakening among the people.

Nehemiah 8:1-12 has a clear emphasis on "the people," mentioned 11 times in this passage. The emphasis is on the people being assembled as a unified body with a common purpose. Every seven years, during the seventh month, God's law was to be read aloud to the people in conjunction with the Feast of Booths (see Neh. 7:73b and Deut. 31:10-12). An outdoor public meeting provided the setting for the reading, hearing, explanation, and application of God's Word. It's one of the earliest revivals in recorded history.

> *"CAN WE RESOLVE TO REACH, LEARN, AND TRY TO HEED THE GREATEST MESSAGE EVER WRITTEN—GOD'S WORD AND THE HOLY BIBLE? INSIDE ITS PAGES LIE ALL THE ANSWERS TO ALL THE PROBLEMS THAT MAN HAS EVER KNOWN."*
> —Ronald Reagan

▶ NEHEMIAH 8:1-12

1 All the people gathered together at the square in front of the Water Gate. They asked Ezra the scribe to bring the book of the law of Moses that the LORD had given Israel. **2** On the first day of the seventh month, Ezra the priest brought the law before the assembly of men, women, and all who could listen with understanding. **3** While he was facing the square in front of the Water Gate, he read out of it from daybreak until noon before the men, the women, and those who could understand. All the people listened attentively to the book of the law. **4** Ezra the scribe stood on a high wooden platform made for this purpose. Mattithiah, Shema, Anaiah, Uriah, Hilkiah, and Maaseiah stood beside him on his right; to his left were Pedaiah, Mishael, Malchijah, Hashum, Hashbaddanah, Zechariah, and Meshullam. **5** Ezra opened the book in full view of all the people, since he was elevated above everyone. As he opened it, all the people stood up. **6** Ezra praised the LORD, the great God, and with their hands uplifted all the people said, "Amen, Amen!" Then they bowed down and worshiped the LORD with their faces to the ground. **7** Jeshua, Bani, Sherebiah, Jamin, Akkub, Shabbethai, Hodiah, Maaseiah, Kelita, Azariah, Jozabad, Hanan, and Pelaiah, who were Levites, explained the law to the people as they stood in their places. **8** They read out of the book of the law of God, translating and giving the meaning so that the people could understand what was read. **9** Nehemiah the governor, Ezra the priest and scribe, and the Levites who were instructing the people said to all of them, "This day is holy to the LORD your God. Do not mourn or weep." For all the people were weeping as they heard the words of the law. **10** Then he said to them, "Go and eat what is rich, drink what is sweet, and send portions to those who have nothing prepared, since today is holy to our Lord. Do not grieve, because the joy of the LORD is your stronghold." **11** And the Levites quieted all the people, saying, "Be still, since today is holy. Do not grieve." **12** Then all the people began to eat and drink, send portions, and have a great celebration, because they had understood the words that were explained to them.

Think About It

Circle references to Old Testament Scriptures in these verses.

Underline all action words that describe how Scripture was handled.

List the people's responses to the Scriptures.

❯ EXPLORE THE TEXT

DESIRE THE WORD (Read Nehemiah 8:1-3.)

The first day of the seventh month was a celebration of the new year in ancient Jerusalem. So the gathering of all the people to the plaza, or square, in front of the Water Gate may have been spontaneous. Impromptu or not, the people of Jerusalem longed to hear God's Word. In this case God's Word meant the law (the first five books of the Old Testament). These books, also known as the Torah, formed the very foundation of Jewish faith and life.

The people called for Ezra to bring God's law and read it to them. Here was a scribe and teacher whose passion in life was to help others know the law of God (see Ezra 7:10). He grabbed the scrolls and hurried to the Water Gate.

The crowd who gathered to hear the law included men, women, and perhaps older children and young adults. The phrase "all who could listen with understanding" (Neh. 8:2) indicates that the people didn't merely desire to hear Ezra read; they wanted to understand the Scriptures. They longed to grasp their meaning and application. The people anticipated that the Scriptures would call them to obedience.

What reaction would you have if a group of people asked you to read and explain God's Word to them?

Ezra read God's law to the residents of Jerusalem. Nehemiah 8:3 indicates that he read in the book from daybreak until noon—that is, for about six hours. Equally amazing is the fact that all the people listened attentively the entire time. It showed their hunger to hear and understand God's Word. The Scriptures were nothing less than God's answers to all their problems (see Ps. 19:7-11).

How would you rate your desire to read (or hear) the Bible?

0   1   2   3   4   5   6   7   8   9   **10**

Seldom desire   Desire daily

What are some ways the Bible helps you daily?

PREPARE TO HEAR (Read Nehemiah 8:4-8.)

So that all the people could hear him, Ezra stood on a high platform built for such an occasion. He was joined on the platform by 13 other men who may have been either priests or influential community leaders. Their roles aren't specified, but their presence on the platform showed they understood the significance of the event.

The crowd showed their reverence to God and eagerness to hear from Him by standing when Ezra opened the book. They knew they weren't just hearing a man speak; they were hearing God's Word.

How can Christ followers today show reverence for the reading of God's Word?

Ezra was so moved by the people's standing response that he uttered a message of praise to God, using God's sacred covenant name, the Lord. On hearing Ezra praise God, the people were stirred in their hearts even more. They lifted their hands high in the air, shouted "Amen! Amen!" (8:6), meaning "Yes! May it be so!" and then bowed down with their faces to the ground. It was a posture of deep humility and surrender before God. By responding in this way, the people showed their submission to the authority of Scripture. They desperately longed to hear God's Word, to pledge themselves to it, and to obey it.

Another group of 13 more helpers (all Levites) had spread out among the crowd. Their role was to help the people understand what they had heard. This responsibility included two activities.

1. The Levites reread passages to ensure that the people had correctly heard Ezra's reading. It was a chance to reinforce the passage. But it was also an opportunity for the instructors to translate the passage into the hearers' everyday language. The law was written in Hebrew, but by Ezra's time many Jews spoke Aramaic, a similar yet distinct language.

2. The Levites helped the people understand the meaning of the biblical readings. They interpreted the Scriptures and explained how God's Word applies in everyday life. They gave the people a verbal picture of faithfulness and obedient living.

List the names of people who've helped you understand and obey God's Word along the way.

List the names of people in your life whom you might help understand God's Word.

MOVE BEYOND LISTENING (Read Nehemiah 8:9-12.)

Here we find clear evidence that Nehemiah and Ezra worked together for a period of time in the restored Jewish community. These two godly leaders, along with the Levite helpers, recognized the significance of the events unfolding near the Water Gate. It was a great awakening of God's people—a day to celebrate with joy.

The years the Jewish people spent in exile had been the result of their spiritual rebellion. Even in the early years of their return, the people had been lax in obeying God's law. When Ezra read the law to them and the Levites explained it, their hearts were pricked. Tears flowed as the people admitted their guilt before God. They repented, and God restored them (see Ex. 34:6-7). Consequently, Nehemiah and Ezra called on the people to rejoice.

The phrase "he said" (Neh. 8:10) can refer to either Ezra or Nehemiah as the primary speaker. Both men (and the Levites) called for the people to celebrate the renewal of their commitment to God. The celebration was to be community-wide, with families who had already prepared rich delicacies sharing with families who had not.

This was a day for the people to focus on God and be refreshed in the joy only He can give. Such joy was their strength, their stronghold during good times or bad. The people did as instructed. Their lives had been changed. They had heard and understood God's Word as never before. Consequently, they had reason to celebrate and rejoice together as the people of God.

How does your joy in the Lord provide strength and refuge during difficult days?

BIBLE SKILL
Examine ways a phrase is used in Scripture.

Focus on the phrase "Amen, Amen!" in Nehemiah 8:6. Read Deuteronomy 27:14-26; 1 Kings 1:36; 1 Chronicles 16:36; and Jeremiah 28:6 to gain a better understanding of how this word was used.

How does the use of this word in the Old Testament compare to the way we use it today?

❯ OBEY THE TEXT

God's people grow in faith by gathering to hear and understand God's Word. Reading Scripture includes seeking to understand the passages and acting on that understanding.

What are you doing individually to regularly place yourself in a position to hear and obey God's Word?

List specific ways you can help new people become involved in Bible study, either in your group or in a new group.

How often do you act on what you're learning through Bible study? What steps does your group need to take to keep one another accountable for applying God's Word?

MEMORIZE

"They read out of the book of the law of God, translating and giving the meaning so that the people could understand what was read" (Neh. 8:8).

Use the space provided to make observations and record prayer requests during the group experience for this session.

MY THOUGHTS

Record insights and questions from the group experience.

_____
_____
_____
_____
_____
_____

MY RESPONSE

Note specific ways you will put into practice the truth explored this week.

_____
_____
_____
_____
_____

MY PRAYERS

List specific prayer needs and answers to remember this week.

_____
_____
_____
_____
_____
_____

COMMIT YOUR WAY TO THE LORD

God expects His people to always be in a process of transformation.

〉 UNDERSTAND THE CONTEXT

ARE YOU TYPICALLY A CONFORMER, A REFORMER, OR A TRANSFORMER?

A conformer acts in accordance with a group's prevailing standards, attitudes, and practices. A reformer seeks to improve on the prevailing standards, attitudes, and practices—especially by correcting abuses. But a transformer seeks to start over, to make a complete change from the inside out so that, in effect, a new person or group emerges with new standards, attitudes, and practices.

God is in the transforming business. He gave Israel the law so that His people would display a distinctive lifestyle—one that reflected His holy character. But because of sin, humankind needed more than a set of guidelines. We needed a change from the inside out. We needed to be transformed. That's why the law ultimately pointed God's people to Jesus Christ (see Gal. 3:22-26). Only through faith in Christ can we become a transformed people who grow to be more like Him in every area of our lives (see 2 Cor. 5:17).

Following the great assembly of repentance and renewal described in Nehemiah 9:1-37, the people of Jerusalem rededicated themselves to live in obedience to God's law (see 9:38–10:39). They expressed their commitment by signing and sealing a document that outlined specific areas of concern. They promised not to neglect those areas again.

Chapters 11–12 contain various reports, lists, and records of events that don't necessarily fall in chronological order. These chapters include the report of Nehemiah's plan to repopulate Jerusalem (see 11:1-2), a list of families who settled in the city (see 11:3-21), a report (or reports) on Levites and priests and a list of villages where Jewish families settled (see 11:22–12:26), a record of the wall-dedication ceremony (see 12:27-43), and a notation about the people's support of the Levites (see 12:44-47).

In chapter 13 the book closes by outlining Nehemiah's second period of service in Jerusalem. After 12 years and a completed mission, Nehemiah had returned to his job as cupbearer to the king of Persia (see 13:6). Sometime later, however, he requested and was granted a leave of absence to visit Jerusalem again. To his dismay, he found that some of the people had lapsed into disobedience. Nehemiah again led the people in correcting all these situations. He prayed for God to remember his acts of faithfulness.

> *"ONE ACT OF OBEDIENCE IS BETTER THAN ONE HUNDRED SERMONS."*
> *—Dietrich Bonhoeffer*

NEHEMIAH 10:28-39

28 The rest of the people—the priests, Levites, gatekeepers, singers, and temple servants, along with their wives, sons, and daughters, everyone who is able to understand and who has separated themselves from the surrounding peoples to obey the law of God— **29** join with their noble brothers and commit themselves with a sworn oath to follow the law of God given through God's servant Moses and to carefully obey all the commands, ordinances, and statutes of Yahweh our Lord. **30** We will not give our daughters in marriage to the surrounding peoples and will not take their daughters as wives for our sons. **31** When the surrounding peoples bring merchandise or any kind of grain to sell on the Sabbath day, we will not buy from them on the Sabbath or a holy day. We will also leave the land uncultivated in the seventh year and will cancel every debt. **32** We will impose the following commands on ourselves: To give an eighth of an ounce of silver yearly for the service of the house of our God: **33** the bread displayed before the LORD, the daily grain offering, the regular burnt offering, the Sabbath and New Moon offerings, the appointed festivals, the holy things, the sin offerings to atone for Israel, and for all the work of the house of our God. **34** We have cast lots among the priests, Levites, and people for the donation of wood by our ancestral houses at the appointed times each year. They are to bring the wood to our God's house to burn on the altar of the LORD our God, as it is written in the law. **35** We will bring the firstfruits of our land and of every fruit tree to the LORD's house year by year. **36** We will also bring the firstborn of our sons and our livestock, as prescribed by the law, and will bring the firstborn of our herds and flocks to the house of our God, to the priests who serve in our God's house. **37** We will bring a loaf from our first batch of dough to the priests at the storerooms of the house of our God. We will also bring the firstfruits of our grain offerings, of every fruit tree, and of the new wine and oil. A tenth of our land's produce belongs to the Levites, for the Levites are to collect the one-tenth offering in all our agricultural towns. **38** A priest of Aaronic descent must accompany the Levites when they collect the tenth, and the Levites must take a tenth of this offering to the storerooms of the treasury in the house of our God. **39** For the Israelites and the Levites are to bring the contributions of grain, new wine, and oil to the storerooms where the articles of the sanctuary are kept and where the priests who minister are, along with the gatekeepers and singers. We will not neglect the house of our God.

Think About It

Circle verses that express the people's commitment to obey God's Word in the following areas of life (some verses may fit in more than one area):

> *Finances*

> *Land management*

> *Worship*

> *Ministry support*

> *Marriage*

> *Work*

> *Parenting*

❯ EXPLORE THE TEXT

COMMITMENT MADE
(Read Nehemiah 10:28-29.)

When scores of Jewish leaders joined Nehemiah in signing a written pledge to obey God's law, the rest of the people also committed themselves to the cause. All the members of the covenant community—priests and temple servants, men and women, young and old—understood the commitment they were making to God. They understood the practical implications of God's call to be separate from the pagan groups living around them. Obedience at times would require them to make difficult choices about relationships or participation in activities. Lastly, they understood the seriousness of their vow. The covenant carried not only the promise of blessings for obedience but also the certainty of curses for disobedience (see Deut. 30:1-3).

When has your commitment to Jesus Christ required separation from other individuals or groups?

HOLINESS SOUGHT *(Read Nehemiah 10:30.)*

In a culture that cherishes individual freedom, it can be a challenge to appreciate ancient marriage practices. Marriages at that time were arranged by a couple's parents, sometimes years before the wedding took place. Marriage was literally a family decision; it bound together two families—not just the bride and groom—in a relationship of shared values, attitudes, and activities.

This is the reason God warned His people in Nehemiah's day not to give their sons and daughters in marriage to non-Jewish families in the land. The issue wasn't so much about ethnic differences as about deeper spiritual differences. God's people were to worship the Lord exclusively, and they were to display His holy character by keeping His commands. Marrying into non-Jewish families would almost certainly result in spiritual compromise. Moreover, the land God gave exclusively to Israel could eventually become the inheritance of an idol-worshiping people.

The people of Jerusalem pledged to obey God's instruction about purity in marriage. Sadly, some of them later faltered in that commitment. Nehemiah then had to rebuke the offenders and call them to return to obedience (see 13:23-31).

Compare 2 Corinthians 6:14-15 to Nehemiah 10:30. What other relationships besides marriage could God's warning about spiritual compromise apply to?

WORSHIP PLEDGED (Read Nehemiah 10:31-39.)

Another area in which the revived covenant people pledged to obey God's law involved worship practices. Because the law contained specific instructions for worship, the people made specific promises of obedience.

Keeping the Sabbath Day was as basic to Israel's life as the fact of creation. That is, God set the pattern when He rested from His work of creation on the seventh day. He blessed the day and declared it to be holy (see Gen. 2:1-3). He then wove this Sabbath principle into the fabric of Israel's life through the Fourth Commandment (see Ex. 20:8-11; Deut. 5:12-15). The Sabbath was to be kept as a day to worship God, to enjoy rest, to help others, and to declare truth.

By Nehemiah's time a merchant economy had developed around the world. Non-Jewish merchants held little or no appreciation for the Sabbath, so they opened their markets to buy and sell on that day just as they did on any other day. The Jews might not be able to control the merchants' actions, but they could choose not to buy or sell from them on the Sabbath Day. As God's people, they pledged to keep the Sabbath holy even when others didn't.

Other applications of the Sabbath principle called for the people to let cultivated land rest every seventh year and to cancel debts after seven years. These practical applications of God's Word served to remind the people that God owned everything and that He was their ultimate and faithful Provider.

What are some specific ways Christ followers today can obey the Sabbath principle?

To what extent should believers resist cultural attitudes and practices that compromise their worship gatherings?

KEY DOCTRINE
Stewardship

Christians should contribute of their means cheerfully, regularly, systematically, proportionately, and liberally for the advancement of the Redeemer's cause on earth.

Next, the people made important commitments that might be referred to as stewardship pledges. They promised to provide for the needs and work of the house of God. The temple in Nehemiah's day required support—financial and otherwise. Therefore, the people pledged to regularly give money for the ongoing support of the temple and its activities. Those activities, spelled out in Nehemiah 10:33, include providing the showbread; making the daily, seasonal, and special offerings; and maintaining the temple building.

Priests kept a fire going at all times for making burnt offerings. Therefore, the people committed to shoulder some of the load in providing the wood. Not everyone could be a priest or Levite or could donate lambs or oxen for sacrifices. But everyone could help in providing the wood, although wood for burning was not a plentiful resource in Israel. The various tribal families joined the priests and Levites to develop a wood-donation schedule.

Giving one's firstfruits to the Lord held powerful symbolism. Firstfruits weren't merely the earliest items to be harvested; they were the choice products, the best the people had to offer (see Ex. 23:19a). By giving their firstfruits at the temple, worshipers not only helped provide for the priests but also showed their belief that God is the Source of all good things and is worthy of everyone's very best.

The firstfruits principle applied in other areas of life as well. The dedication to the Lord of firstborn sons and the firstborn of all livestock harkened back to the time of the exodus. It was a dramatic reminder of the price that was paid to rescue the Israelites from bondage in Egypt (see Ex. 13:11-16). Even more poignantly, it was a powerful foreshadowing of the redemption from sin that comes through Jesus Christ. In Jesus, God gave His one and only Son—His very best—so that those who believe in Jesus won't perish in their sins but will receive everlasting life (see John 3:16; 1 Pet. 1:18-21).

These verses describe the Jews' commitment to bring offerings and tithes to the storehouse—that is, to the temple (see Mal. 3:10). The law provided for the Levites to be supported by a tithe, since they as a group weren't given an inheritance of land (see Num. 18:21-24). Still, even the Levites were to give a tenth of their income to support the work of the temple (see 18:26). In other words, as the people tithed to the Levites, the Levites in turn tithed to the priests at the temple. The injunction that a priest from the lineage of Aaron must accompany the Levites in their collection of support helped ensure against the possibility or accusation of improperly handling funds.

God's house was to be respected, honored, and sustained. All of God's people can and should do their part to support and advance the work of God's kingdom locally and worldwide.

In what ways can people demonstrate obedience to the Lord through their worship?

BIBLE SKILL
Analyze passages on a topic to gain a clear understanding of a practice.

Nehemiah challenged the Jews to make a regular practice of supporting God's work through tithes and offerings. Read Genesis 14:20; Leviticus 27:30-32; Numbers 18:20-32; Deuteronomy 12:4-6; Proverbs 3:9; Malachi 3:8-12; Matthew 23:23; and Mark 12:41-44. Write a summary sentence, based on these passages, of the expectations God has for His people relative to tithes and offerings.

❯ OBEY THE TEXT

Believers desire to obey God's Word in all areas of their lives. God expects His people to live a life characterized by holiness. Sincere worship is one way believers demonstrate their love for God.

On a scale of 1 to 10, with 10 being fully obedient, rate your willingness to obey God in all areas of your life. What areas keep you from rating yourself higher? What do you need to do to begin obeying God more in any areas of disobedience?

What could you point to in your life as evidence that you're seeking to live a God-honoring life? Ask a trusted friend to evaluate the evidence. What needs to change this week for you to grow in honoring God?

As a group, identify attitudes, practices, and actions demonstrating that someone is committed to worship. How can the group hold one another accountable for the items included on the list?

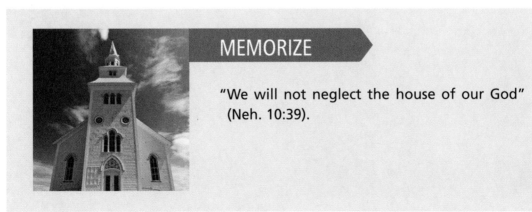

MEMORIZE

"We will not neglect the house of our God" (Neh. 10:39).

Use the space provided to make observations and record prayer requests during the group experience for this session.

MY THOUGHTS
Record insights and questions from the group experience.

_____

_____

_____

_____

_____

_____

MY RESPONSE
Note specific ways you will put into practice the truth explored this week.

_____

_____

_____

_____

_____

_____

MY PRAYERS
List specific prayer needs and answers to remember this week.

_____

_____

_____

_____

_____

_____

❯ GETTING STARTED

OPENING OPTIONS: Choose one of the following to open the group discussion.

WEEKLY QUOTATION DISCUSSION STARTER: "When God searches for a man to advance His kingdom, does He call your name?"—Dr. Tony Evans

> ❯ What's your initial response to this week's quotation?

> ❯ If God made you aware of something, even during this study of the Book of Nehemiah, would you follow His lead if it changed the direction of your life? Why or why not?

CREATIVE ACTIVITY: Prior to the group gathering, identify a song that gets stuck in your head. It may be annoying or pleasantly memorable. You may want to play a clip of that song for your group. Ask members to identify favorite or least favorite songs that get stuck in their heads. (If this is anyone's first time meeting with your group, have members introduce themselves before sharing their answers). Have members vote on the catchiest or most annoying song of all time. Use the following questions to open the group discussion.

> ❯ When a song gets stuck in your head, you have only two choices: Do you sing along, or do you try to forget it? What do you do when you want to get the song out of your mind?

> ❯ Some things can't be unheard. In Nehemiah 1 a man is told news that troubles him to the depths of his heart and mind, changing the direction of his life forever. Have you ever been made aware of a problem, big or small, that you knew you had to either intentionally ignore or do something about? What did you do?

❯ UNDERSTAND THE CONTEXT

PROVIDE BACKGROUND: Briefly introduce members to the Book of Nehemiah by pointing out the major themes and any information or ideas that will help them understand Nehemiah 2:1-8,17-18. Then, to help them personally connect today's context with the original context, ask the following questions.

> ❯ Nehemiah felt a burden for the city of his ancestors—God's people in Jerusalem. How were geography, political kingdoms, and worship more intertwined in Nehemiah's time than today?

> ❯ Why is it important to remember that we're part of a larger community of faith and a bigger story than just our own?

❯ EXPLORE THE TEXT

READ THE BIBLE: Ask a volunteer to read aloud Nehemiah 2:1-8,17-18.

DISCUSS: Use the following questions to discuss group members' initial reactions to the text.

> ❯ What problem did God's people face? Why was it an important matter?

> ❯ What do these verses reveal about Nehemiah's character?

> ❯ How were Nehemiah's reputation and position in the king's court useful for God's purpose?

> ❯ Why is it significant that Nehemiah "prayed to the God of heaven" (v. 4) before acting?

> ❯ Why is it significant that Nehemiah credited being "graciously strengthened by my God" (v. 8) and "the gracious hand of my God" (v. 18) for his favor with the king?

> ❯ Why is it significant that Nehemiah made specific requests of the king? What did he request?

> ❯ What do you like best about these verses? What questions do you have?

NOTE: Provide ample time for group members to share responses and questions about the text. Don't feel pressured to prioritize the printed agenda over group members' personal experiences. If time allows, discuss responses to the questions in the personal reading.

❯ OBEY THE TEXT

RESPOND: Foster an environment of openness and action. Help individuals apply biblical truth to specific areas of personal thought, attitude, and/or behavior.

> ❯ When was the last time you felt a burden for others—one that drove you to prayer and action?

> ❯ What needs are you aware of among God's people today? How has God positioned you to make a difference?

> ❯ Is there anything you know God has put on your heart that you've been afraid to do or even pray about? How can this group encourage you to follow God's direction?

> ❯ How will you commit to pray for godly wisdom?

PRAY: Close by asking God to give you a deep passion for His work. Pray for an awareness of the needs around you and of how God has uniquely positioned you to make a difference. Humbly follow Nehemiah's example by asking God for clear, specific action steps.

For helps on how to use *Explore The Bible*, tips on how to better lead groups, or additional ideas for leading, visit: **www.ministrygrid.com/web/ExploreTheBible.**

❯ GETTING STARTED

OPENING OPTIONS: Choose one of the following to open the group discussion.

WEEKLY QUOTATION DISCUSSION STARTER: "Forgiveness is not pretending like it didn't happen or like it didn't hurt. That's called lying. Forgiveness is a decision to release a debt regardless of how you feel."—Dr. Tony Evans

> ❯ What's your initial response to this week's quotation?

> ❯ Today we'll look at unity and justice. Why is acknowledging hurt a step toward healing and long-term health (both personally and relationally)?

CREATIVE ACTIVITY: Prior to the group gathering, prepare by finding examples of social-justice or charity causes in popular culture (for example, fair-trade, environmental-protection, or education labels on groceries; businesses donating proceeds to charitable causes; community events to raise awareness and funds for medical research). Use the following questions to open the group discussion.

> ❯ Do you think the popularity of social and charitable causes has increased in our culture? Why or why not?

> ❯ Today we'll look at the reputation and behavior of God's people. Are Christians viewed as more interested than the general public, less interested than the general public, or equally interested as the general public in matters of justice?

❯ UNDERSTAND THE CONTEXT

PROVIDE BACKGROUND: Briefly introduce group members to any information or ideas that will help them understand Nehemiah 5:1-13. Then, to help them personally connect today's context with the original context, ask the following questions.

> ❯ God's people had endured many hardships at the hands of their enemies, but then they took advantage of one another. How do people try to justify getting what they want at someone else's expense?

> ❯ There are many problems in the world. Why is it important for God's people to be united and distinct in our love for others?

❯ EXPLORE THE TEXT

READ THE BIBLE: Ask a volunteer to read aloud Nehemiah 5:1-13.

DISCUSS: Use the following questions to discuss group members' initial reactions to the text.

> How would you describe the injustice God's people were inflicting on one another?

> What reasons did Nehemiah give for confronting injustice?

> Why is it significant that Nehemiah led by example? How did he not only bring attention to a problem but also invite others to join him in the solution?

> What responses did the oppressors and oppressed have to Nehemiah's act of bold compassion? How were the people of God unified?

> What do you like best about these verses? What questions do you have?

NOTE: Provide ample time for group members to share responses and questions about the text. Don't feel pressured to prioritize the printed agenda over group members' personal experiences. If time allows, discuss responses to the questions in the personal reading.

❯ OBEY THE TEXT

RESPOND: Foster an environment of openness and action. Help individuals apply biblical truth to specific areas of personal thought, attitude, and/or behavior.

> Whom have you wronged and need to ask forgiveness?

> How can you encourage unity in your community? In your church?

> For what injustice are you most passionate about being part of the solution? How do you seek to lead by example, raising awareness and living sacrificially?

PRAY: Close by praying for the strength to forgive others and to do everything in your power to make things right. Using Nehemiah's example of shaking out his robe, ask God to free you from deep or hidden sin so that you can spend your life loving Him and loving others.

❯ GETTING STARTED

OPENING OPTIONS: Choose one of the following to open the group discussion.

WEEKLY QUOTATION DISCUSSION STARTER: "Never be afraid to trust an unknown future to a known God."—Corrie Ten Boom

> ❯ What's your initial response to this week's quotation?

> ❯ Today we'll look at remaining confident in God's calling regardless of your current situation. When have you felt sure of God's presence or blessing? When have you been able to see how God was at work after going through a time when you felt that He was far away?

CREATIVE ACTIVITY: Prior to the group gathering, prepare by printing several pictures of easily recognizable images (for example, team or brand logos, celebrity faces, movie posters or album covers, depending on your group's interests). Cut at least half the image away, leaving only one small but still recognizable piece of each image to show group members. Vary the size of the piece you'll show for each image. Display each image and give everyone a moment to think about it. Use the following questions with each image to open discussion.

> ❯ Who is confident they can accurately identify this image? Who or what is it?

> ❯ What characteristic helped you recognize this image even without seeing the full picture?

After showing all the images, ask the following question to transition to your study.

> ❯ When have you had to trust what you knew about God in a situation, even though He was hard to see?

❯ UNDERSTAND THE CONTEXT

PROVIDE BACKGROUND: Briefly introduce group members to any information or ideas that will help them understand Nehemiah 6:1-19. Then, to help them personally connect today's context with the original context, ask the following questions.

> ❯ Why would non-Israelite officials oppose Nehemiah and the work to rebuild Jerusalem?

> ❯ What resistance do people face today for doing God's work in our culture and around the world?

70 EXPLORE THE BIBLE

❯ EXPLORE THE TEXT

READ THE BIBLE: Ask a volunteer to read aloud Nehemiah 6:1-19.

DISCUSS: Use the following questions to discuss group members' initial reactions to the text.

> How would you describe the conflict in this passage?

> What strategies were used to intimidate, discourage, deceive, and even harm Nehemiah?

> What specific responses did Nehemiah have to opposition? Why are the things Nehemiah focused on significant when he was challenged and tempted?

> What was the result of Nehemiah's faithfulness in adversity?

> What do you like best about these verses? What questions do you have?

NOTE: Provide ample time for group members to share responses and questions about the text. Don't feel pressured to prioritize the printed agenda over group members' personal experiences. If time allows, discuss responses to the questions in the personal reading.

❯ OBEY THE TEXT

RESPOND: Foster an environment of openness and action. Help individuals apply biblical truth to specific areas of personal thought, attitude, and/or behavior.

> What struggle are you facing now?

> How can we encourage you to remain faithful to God's work in your life?

PRAY: Close by praying for faithfulness in adversity. If time allows and if your group is comfortable with doing so, have group members pray in pairs for specific areas of struggle, temptation, or hardship. Otherwise, ask for any specific areas of struggle, temptation, or hardship for which people would like to request prayer and close with a prayer for your group members.

❯ GETTING STARTED

OPENING OPTIONS: Choose one of the following to open the group discussion.

WEEKLY QUOTATION DISCUSSION STARTER: "The greatest player on any team, whether a corporate, family, ministry, or sports team, is the player who makes certain that his contribution best fits within the goals and strategies of the team."—Dr. Tony Evans

> ❯ What's your initial response to this week's quotation?

> ❯ How would you describe God's goal in the world? His strategy?

CREATIVE ACTIVITY: Prior to the group gathering, prepare or purchase a treat. Divide the treat in half and noticeably alter the flavor of one half (by adding too much salt, for example). After people react to the bad treat, provide the good treat. Use the following questions to open the group discussion.

> ❯ What was wrong with the first treat?

> ❯ When else have you had too much of a good thing?

> ❯ Today we'll look at cooperation. What are some examples in life when proper teamwork or balance is critical to a good outcome?

❯ UNDERSTAND THE CONTEXT

PROVIDE BACKGROUND: Briefly introduce group members to any information or ideas that will help them understand Nehemiah 7:1-7a. Then, to help them personally connect today's context with the original context, ask the following questions.

> ❯ How have you experienced the benefit of everyone's working together toward a common goal?

> ❯ How can shared responsibility be valuable in the church today?

❯ EXPLORE THE TEXT

READ THE BIBLE: Ask a volunteer to read aloud Nehemiah 7:1-7a.

DISCUSS: Use the following questions to discuss group members' initial reactions to the text.

> How would you describe the need Nehemiah identified after the wall had been rebuilt?

> What did Nehemiah do to build community, not just a city wall? How did these actions show wisdom as a leader?

> What criteria did Nehemiah use in assigning personal responsibilities? Why are those things important in building community?

> Where did Nehemiah get the idea to assemble and register all the people? Why was the origin of that idea significant? How could the result of that process be significant?

> What do you like best about these verses? What questions do you have?

NOTE: Provide ample time for group members to share responses and questions about the text. Don't feel pressured to prioritize the printed agenda over group members' personal experiences. If time allows, discuss responses to the questions in the personal reading.

❯ OBEY THE TEXT

RESPOND: Foster an environment of openness and action. Help individuals apply biblical truth to specific areas of personal thought, attitude, and/or behavior.

> What are you currently doing to serve in God's work?

> What's the difference between doing a project and building community?

> What specific responsibility will you share this week? Whom will you invite to build meaningful community with?

> How will you be an encourager this week?

PRAY: Close by asking someone to lead the group in prayer. Encourage this member to pray for everyone to seek ways to join God's work this week.

> GETTING STARTED

OPENING OPTIONS: Choose one of the following to open your group discussion.

WEEKLY QUOTATION DISCUSSION STARTER: "Can we resolve to reach, learn, and try to heed the greatest message ever written—God's Word and the Holy Bible? Inside its pages lie all the answers to all the problems that man has ever known."—Ronald Reagan

> ❯ What's your initial response to this week's quotation?

> ❯ If other people looked at your life, what conclusion would they come to about the Bible— its origin, value, and purpose?

CREATIVE ACTIVITY: When the group has gathered, begin by reading aloud the following phrases: "This too shall pass." "God helps those who help themselves." "Cleanliness is next to godliness." "God works in mysterious ways." "If you believe it, you can achieve it." "Let go and let God." Explain that phrases like these are sometimes attributed to the Bible, but none of them are actually Bible verses. Use the following questions to open the group discussion.

> ❯ Although some of these popular phrases are more true or valuable than others, why is it important to recognize what actually is and isn't in the Bible?

> ❯ What's one of your favorite verses, stories, or truths from God's Word and why?

> UNDERSTAND THE CONTEXT

PROVIDE BACKGROUND: Briefly introduce group members to any information or ideas that will help them understand Nehemiah 8:1-12. Then, to help them personally connect today's context with the original context, ask the following questions.

> ❯ God's people had returned from exile, had rebuilt Jerusalem's wall, and had begun reestablishing community. Why was it still vital to reintroduce individuals to the Word of God?

> ❯ What's the danger when people do good things without a personal relationship with God?

❯ EXPLORE THE TEXT

READ THE BIBLE: Ask a volunteer to read aloud Nehemiah 8:1-12.

DISCUSS: Use the following questions to discuss group members' initial reactions to the text.

> What need was met in this chapter?

> Why was it significant that God's Word was read to "men, women and all who could listen with understanding" (v. 2) and "in full view of all the people" (v. 5)?

> What did the Levites do after Scripture had been read (vv. 7-8)? Why was this essential?

> What specific phrases are used to describe the different responses of people who heard God's Word? How did Nehemiah and Ezra ultimately direct people to respond?

> What does this text teach about a right understanding of and response to God's Word?

> What do you like best about these verses? What questions do you have?

NOTE: Provide ample time for group members to share responses and questions about the text. Don't feel pressured to prioritize the printed agenda over group members' personal experiences. If time allows, discuss responses to the questions in the personal reading.

❯ OBEY THE TEXT

RESPOND: Foster an environment of openness and action. Help individuals apply biblical truth to specific areas of personal thought, attitude, and/or behavior.

The people asked for God's Word, stood all day attentively listening to it, and responded in emotional and sincere worship. Honestly, how does your attitude toward the Bible compare to theirs?

> What will you do this week to give God and His Word priority in your life?

> How can you help others understand and respond to God's Word?

PRAY: Close by reading aloud Scripture as your prayer. Suggestions include Psalm 23; 51; 63; 86; 139; 145; or Matthew 6:9-13.

❯ GETTING STARTED

OPENING OPTIONS: Choose one of the following to open your group discussion.

WEEKLY QUOTATION DISCUSSION STARTER: "One act of obedience is better than one hundred sermons."—Dietrich Bonhoeffer

> ❯ What's your initial response to this week's quotation?

> ❯ How does knowing that Bonhoeffer was a pastor executed in Nazi Germany add significance to his perspective on both preaching and being committed to a lifestyle of faithfulness?

> ❯ Why is this quotation timely for our final session of this study (or any study)?

CREATIVE ACTIVITY: When the group has gathered, begin by instructing members to balance on one foot. While they balance, use the following questions to open the group discussion.

> ❯ What's the difference between walking and running? (Answer: Walking always has at least one foot on the ground, and both feet are on the ground when completing a step. Running has only one foot on the ground when completing a step, and no feet are on the ground between steps.)

> ❯ You have one foot on the ground now. Are you walking or running? (Answer: obviously not)

> ❯ What's the difference between walking, running, and standing? (Answer: a continual process)

Explain that in this final session we'll see that Christian commitment is both a one-time decision and an ongoing process.

❯ UNDERSTAND THE CONTEXT

PROVIDE BACKGROUND: Briefly introduce group members to any information or ideas that will help them understand Nehemiah 10:28-39. Then, to help them personally connect today's context with the original context, ask the following questions.

> ❯ The emotional response God's people initially had to the law was incomplete without a personal commitment to living according to what it said. How have you experienced initial enthusiasm in any area of life that faded to reveal the true need for commitment?

> ❯ What's the value of emotional moments without ongoing commitment?

❯ EXPLORE THE TEXT

READ THE BIBLE: Ask a volunteer to read aloud Nehemiah 10:28-39.

DISCUSS: Use the following questions to discuss group members' initial reactions to the text.

> What need was met near the end of the account?

> What's significant about the phrase "separated themselves from the surrounding peoples to obey the law of God" (v. 28)? What's significant about committing "to carefully obey all the commands, ordinances, and statutes of Yahweh our Lord" (v. 29)?

> Why is it vital to recognize Scripture as coming through God's servants from "Yahweh our Lord" (v. 29)?

> What practical examples are listed for being a people set apart and governed by God's law?

> What do you like best about these verses? What questions do you have?

> How would you summarize the overall story and point of the Book of Nehemiah? What's been most significant for you in this study of God's Word?

NOTE: Provide ample time for group members to share responses and questions about the text. Don't feel pressured to prioritize the printed agenda over group members' personal experiences. If time allows, discuss responses to the questions in the personal reading.

❯ OBEY THE TEXT

RESPOND: Foster an environment of openness and action. Help individuals apply biblical truth to specific areas of personal thought, attitude, and/or behavior.

> Is your life distinctly set apart for God? What personal encouragement or conviction do you find in this Scripture text?

> What part of the Bible have you lacked commitment to carefully obey? How will you begin to treat the entire Bible as the Word of God—the Lord who's personally committed to you?

> How will you "not neglect the house of our God" (v. 39)?

PRAY: Close with a prayer of commitment and courage to live differently than the culture around you. Thank God for His holiness and grace in Jesus. Ask His Spirit to help you persevere in living for the sake of God's work in the world.

❯TIPS FOR LEADING A GROUP

PRAYERFULLY PREPARE

Prepare for each session by—

> - **reviewing the weekly material and group questions ahead of time;**
> - **praying for each person in the group.**

Ask the Holy Spirit to work through you and the group discussion to help people take steps toward Jesus each week as directed by God's Word.

MINIMIZE DISTRACTIONS

Create a comfortable environment. If group members are uncomfortable, they'll be distracted and therefore not engaged in the group experience. Plan ahead by taking into consideration—

> - **seating;**
> - **temperature;**
> - **lighting;**
> - **food or drink;**
> - **surrounding noise;**
> - **general cleanliness (put pets away if meeting in a home).**

At best, thoughtfulness and hospitality show guests and group members they're welcome and valued in whatever environment you choose to gather. At worst, people may never notice your effort, but they're also not distracted. Do everything in your ability to help people focus on what's most important: connecting with God, with the Bible, and with others.

INCLUDE OTHERS

Your goal is to foster a community in which people are welcome just as they are but encouraged to grow spiritually. Always be aware of opportunities to—

> - **invite** new people to join your group;
> - **include** any people who visit the group.

An inexpensive way to make first-time guests feel welcome or to invite people to get involved is to give them their own copies of this Bible study book.

ENCOURAGE DISCUSSION

A good small group has the following characteristics.

> **Everyone participates.** Encourage everyone to ask questions, share responses, or read aloud.

> **No one dominates—not even the leader.** Be sure what you say takes up less than half of your time together as a group. Politely redirect discussion if anyone dominates.

> **Nobody is rushed through questions.** Don't feel that a moment of silence is a bad thing. People often need time to think about their responses to questions they've just heard or to gain courage to share what God is stirring in their hearts.

> **Input is affirmed and followed up.** Make sure you point out something true or helpful in a response. Don't just move on. Build personal connections with follow-up questions, asking how other people have experienced similar things or how a truth has shaped their understanding of God and the Scripture you're studying. People are less likely to speak up if they fear that you don't actually want to hear their answers or that you're looking for only a certain answer.

> **God and His Word are central.** Opinions and experiences can be helpful, but God has given us the truth. Trust Scripture to be the authority and God's Spirit to work in people's lives. You can't change anyone, but God can. Continually point people to the Word and to active steps of faith.

KEEP CONNECTING

Think of ways to connect with group members during the week. Participation during the group session is always improved when members spend time connecting with one another away from the session. The more people are comfortable with and involved in one another's lives, the more they'll look forward to being together. When people move beyond being friendly and in the same group to truly being friends who form a community, they come to each session eager to engage instead of merely attending.

Encourage group members with thoughts, commitments, or questions from the session by connecting through—

> **emails;**
> **texts;**
> **social media.**

When possible, build deeper friendships by planning or spontaneously inviting group members to join you outside your regularly scheduled group time for—

> **meals;**
> **fun activities;**
> **projects around your home, church, or community.**

❯ GROUP CONTACT INFORMATION

Name _____ Number _____

Email _____

Name _____ Number _____

Email _____

Name _____ Number _____

Email _____

Name _____ Number _____

Email _____

Name _____ Number _____

Email _____

Name _____ Number _____

Email _____

Name _____ Number _____

Email _____

Name _____ Number _____

Email _____

Name _____ Number _____

Email _____

Name _____ Number _____

Email _____

Name _____ Number _____

Email _____